The Christmas Dove & The Woodcutter

by Peter Canwell

Music arranged by
PHILIP EVRY

The Christmas Dove and the Woodcutter mixes fantasy with tradition in a dramatic presentation with music, of events leading up to the Holy Nativity.

Staging requirements are minimal although good lighting plays an important part. Costume and props may be as imaginative as resources permit.

The story is narrated to Hannah and Simon by their grandfather, and this little group should be positioned to one side of the stage.

The choir has an important role and should be placed close to the stage where it can feel fully involved in the production. Unison and easy two-part singing is all that is required although optional fuller harmony is occasionally indicated. The vocal melody is not given a separate stave, but follows the top line (top two lines, where the voices divide) in the piano part. Where this is not the case a dotted continuation line shows the melodic progression. The accompaniment may be varied at the pianist's discretion.

There are opportunities for dance/movement and the part of Silver (the dove) should ideally be taken by a girl with dancing experience.

Exclusive Distributors
International Music Publications Limited
Southend Road, Woodford Green,
Essex IG8 8HN, England.

Taking part

Grandfather (*Narrator*)
Simon (*grandson*)
Hannah (*Simon's younger sister*)
King Herod
Chancellor
Captain of Guard
Marcus (*Herod's slave*)
Silver — the Dove
Woodcutter
Mary
Joseph

The Three Kings
Soldiers
Shepherds
Angels

Crowd in Street scene
Groups representing:
      Thunder
      Lightning
      Snowstorm

CHOIR

CONTENTS

The choir may be used to augment the on-stage singing wherever desirable.

1. Welcome To Judaea

(Crowd and CHOIR)

CUE: (TRUMPET FANFARE)

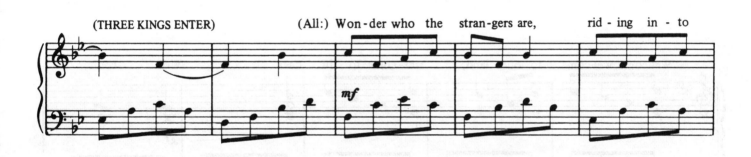

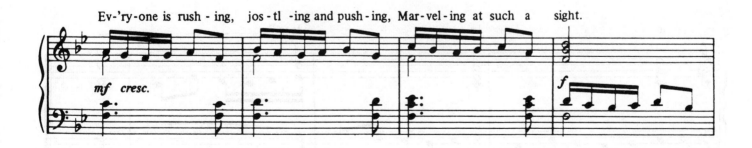

Her - od sends a greet - ing: soon they will be meet - ing; They'll be en - ter - tained to - night.

Great ex - cite - ment ev - 'ry - where, peo - ple shout and cheer,

"Wel - come, wel - come to our land, wel - come to Ju - daea. Wel - come,

wel - come to Ju - daea, Wel - come, wel - come

to Ju - daea."

1a. Reprise - Welcome To Judaea

(Crowd and CHOIR)

CUE: (THE CROWD DIVIDES TO MAKE WAY FOR THE THREE KINGS)

2. Melchior, Caspar And Balthazar

(The Three Kings)

CUE: Let us introduce ourselves to your Majesty.

1. I'm Mel - chi-or, I'm Cas - par and I am Bal - tha -
2. East -ern kings, Lord Her - rod, and we have journ-eyed
3. King is born, Lord Her - rod, the great - est King of

-zar; _____ Three kings we come a - rid - ing, fol - low-ing a
far, _____ To find a child, the Son of God, guid - ed by a
all. _____ His home is not a pal - ace, but a cat - tle

star. _____ Just fol - low-ing, just fol - low-ing a
star. _____ We're fol - low-ing, we're fol - low-ing a
stall. _____ The great - est King, the great - est King of

star.   2. We're
star.   3. A
all!   4. I'm

5

3. Who Is This Child?

(Herod, Captain)

CUE: Do not fail me.

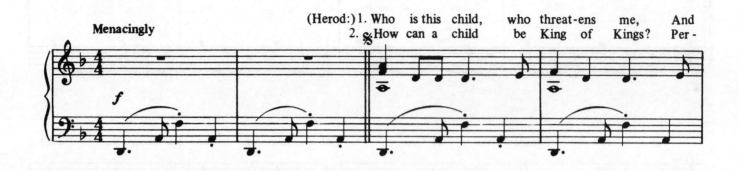

(Herod:) 1. Who is this child, who threat-ens me, And
2. How can a child be King of Kings? Per-

where is this child to - night? And why do they call him the
-haps it is all a lie! But I can - not rest while this

To Coda ⊕

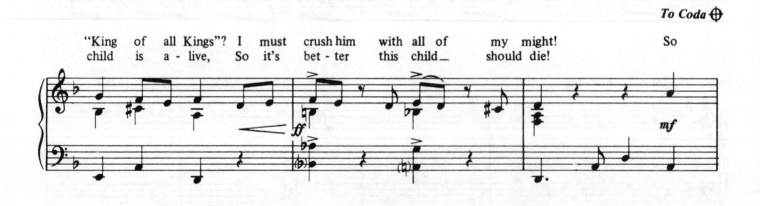

"King of all Kings"? I must crush him with all of my might! So
child is a - live, So it's bet - ter this child should die! So

fol - low the kings as they fol - low the star, And re - mem-ber to keep out of sight.

6

7

4. Because Of Him

(Marcus and CHOIR)

CUE: Good luck my friend and return safely.

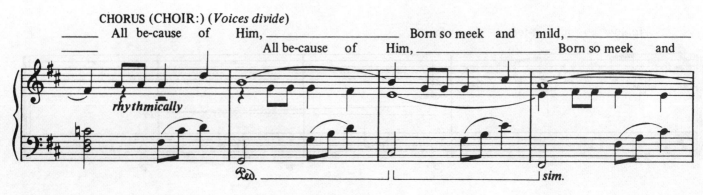

5. The Woodcutter's Prayer

(Woodcutter)

CUE: What I am about to tell you truly happened.

Gently with a lilt

(Woodcutter:) 1. One night three stran-gers I'd not seen be - fore,_____ And all dressed in roy - al robes, stood out - side my door. I off - ered them shel - ter un - til morn - ing light,_____ And when they had rest - ed, we talked through the night. And they told me the sto - ry of their jour - ney far,_____ And how they were foll-ow-ing a

heav - en - ly star.

2. They
3. So

prayer. Yes, I'll make Him a sim-ple gift With such lov - ing care: A

cresc. *f* *dim.*

crib full of gen-tle-ness — A wood - cut - ter's prayer.

rit.

2. They spoke of a baby so soon to be born.
   A child blessed in heaven; the first Christmas morn.
   I sat there and listened to their ev'ry word:
   The loveliest story that I'd ever heard.
   In my heart I believed in Him and longed to be there.
   I knelt down and whispered a woodcutter's prayer.

3. So what can I give Him? A poor man am I.
   The strangers just smiled at me and gave their reply:
   "His home is a stable, this King from a-bove,
   He doesn't want presents, He just wants your love."
   So I'll make Him a simple gift with such loving care:
   A crib full of gentleness — a woodcutter's prayer.
   Yes, I'll make Him a simple gift with such loving care:
   A crib full of gentleness — a woodcutter's prayer.

6.

Find Me My Star
(Woodcutter)

CUE: Away you go . . . . fly free.

14

6a.

Reprise - Find Me My Star

(CHOIR)

CUE: Well done little friend. Lead the way and I'll follow.

Fast and bright

(CHOIR) Fly ov - er o - ceans, ex - plore ev - 'ry shore, And keep on be - liev - ing it's worth search - ing for; So fly on for - ev - er, no mat - ter how far, Re - mem - ber your miss - ion and find me my star.

7. The Angels' Message

(Angels and CHOIR)

CUE: . . . . the shepherds were terrified.(LIGHTS)

With movement

VERSE
(Angels:) 1. Do not fear for

we are from hea - ven; List - en to the mes - sage we bring:

Born this night in Beth - le - hem town, A Ho - ly child: the

CHORUS
Sav - iour King. (Add CHOIR) Glor - i - a, in ex - cel - sis De - o,

2. There He lies asleep in a manger.
   Not for Him a palace and throne,
   But a stable cheerless and empty,
   For the greatest love ever known.
                              CHORUS

3. Leave your sheep and go and adore Him,
   There's a star to show you the way.
   Christ has come, so lift up your voices,
   Welcome Him, on His birth-day.
                              CHORUS

8.   How Do We Get To Bethlehem?

(Shepherds, Angels)

CUE: Have no fear . . . . just follow that star.

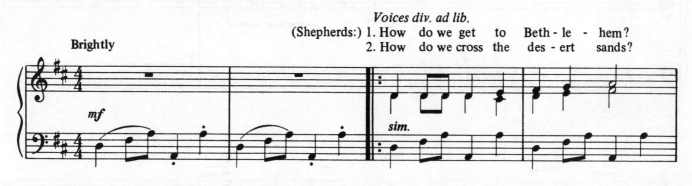

to Beth - le - hem.
to Beth - le - hem.

(Shep-
herds:) 5. What shall we find when we are there? A shin - ing star a - bove the door; Three

(Angels:)

East - ern kings in a sta - ble poor; A new - born child in a cat - tle stall; And

(Shepherds:)

where He sleeps we'll find our sheep. And look a - bove, you'll

(Angels:)

find the dove, In Beth - le - hem.

(All:)

8a. Reprise 1 - How Do We Get To Bethlehem?

(Shepherds)

CUE: Lead the way my little dove.

8b. Reprise 2 - How Do We Get To Bethlehem?

(Shepherds, Woodcutter)

CUE: Oh, I nearly forgot the crib. (PICKS IT UP)

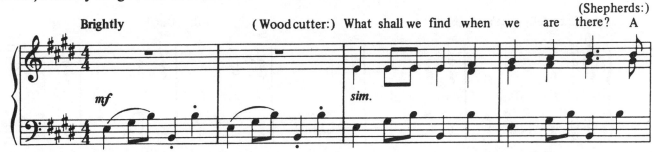

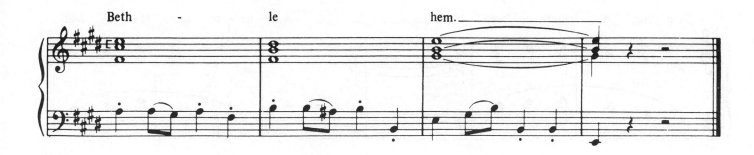

9. Bell Carol

(Cast and CHOIR)

CUE: They too are rejoicing in the birth of this great child.

Come To Bethlehem

(CHOIR)

CUE: Silver saw everything. (LIGHTS UP ON STABLE SCENE)

2. Shepherds hearing the angel voice,
And hurrying to obey,
Find the stable in Bethlehem;
Give praises to God for this Christmas day.

CHORUS:

Come to Bethlehem, to a stable bare.
Come to Bethlehem; SHEPHERDS ALL ARE THERE.

3. Wise men travelling from afar,
Are carrying gifts so rare,
Gold and frankincense, myrhh they bring
And worship this child with a humble prayer.

CHORUS:

Come to Bethlehem, to a stable bare.
Come to Bethlehem; EASTERN KINGS ARE THERE .
Come to Bethlehem, to a stable bare.
Come to Bethlehem; EVERYONE IS THERE,
EVERYONE IS THERE.

11. The Dove's Carol

(Silver)

CUE: (SILVER APPROACHES THE MANGER)

12.   Reprise - Because Of Him

(Marcus and CHOIR)

CUE: (SPOTLIGHT ON MARCUS)

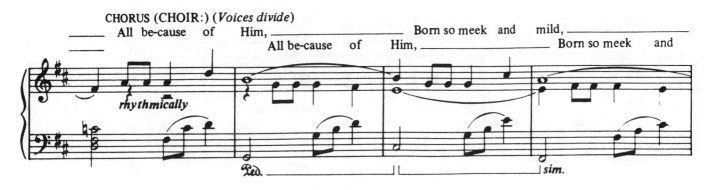

Reproduced and printed by
Halstan & Co. Ltd., Amersham, Bucks., England